CHANGING TIDES

a collection of poems

by
Stanley Josephs

Bombshelter Press
Los Angeles, 2005

First Edition

© Copyright 2005 by Donna and Ira Josephs, Los Angeles, California.

ISBN 0-941017-24-9

Bombshelter Press

P.O. Box 481266, Bicentennial Station, Los Angeles, CA 90048

www.BombshelterPress.com

Contents

For Dad

and
to Marty Krofft,
our father's best friend,
a man who lives the meaning of friendship.

Introduction

The ocean was truly our father's favorite place to be. Away from the busy city, the pressure, and demands. He wrote his beloved poetry in his loft – overlooking the beach in Santa Monica, and at his small wooden desk on the shores of Santa Barbara.

The ocean soothed him, as it does so many – calming and inviting him to touch the infinite, the creative spirit, that poured through his soul.

A dedicated surgeon by day, and a fabulous poet at night and in the early morning hours – his favorite time, his sacred time.

Our father passed away in the prime of his life, snatched away like an unsuspecting fish, grabbed by the mouth of a hungry pelican.

We entitled this book of our father's poems, *Changing Tides*, because of our awareness of how vulnerable we are as we navigate through the ocean of life.

May your journey be sweet, dear reader.

Donna Josephs

Donna wrote a few poems in response to her father's illness and passing.

Proceeds of the sales of this book are going to charities that promote healing.

bio
(written in 1996)

Stan Josephs is an orthopedic surgeon who resides
in Santa Monica, California, and writes poetry when
he is not fixing bones. He started writing because
he wanted to befriend that part of himself that
wandered away when he was young. The part
hidden behind trees, the part that did not see
the sparkle on water in moonlight. His writing
became the wine cask of his beginning, and
when he writes, he knows what he missed,
and slowly sips, one glass at a time, knowing
there is no end to discovery.

untested

How tall do I have to be,
to look over the fence.
To see the ballgame.
The winners and
the losers.
How tall can the grass grow
where deer have walked,
and can it grow again.
Can someone in the past
be loved so much
that love today
can never grow.
Dreams of the future
are never real.
Only the past.
The future is untested
like a new airplane.
Its wings shine
but the wind
howls at the wheels.

patterns

As I drove to the city
I heard a call.
It was the sun
with two voices.
One that dreamed in Navajo.
My friend spoke
about Navajo rugs,
and how he bought one
from an old lady
on her knees
with one tooth
in a tent in New Mexico.
And in this country with
so many cars
I wondered why
she was so removed
and weaving.

for my son who loves animals

He ran from person to person on a summer day.
Entered the house sweating, and breathless.
"Quick, we must call someone to help the seal.
It's still alive." He ran out again, his legs were
thin sticks alighting from oversized shorts. His
arms as long as baseball bats. His hair tossed
to one side of his face, and curled back like a
wave ready to drop. People gathered where he
threw the blanket over the beached mammal.
He phoned for help, but was told they do not
save them, but let nature take its course.
I stayed at the window to watch his effort
to save the animal. It reminded me
of the time we caught a fish together
and how he asked me to toss it back, to let it live
as he wanted this one to live. He waited
explosively, and spoke to all those who walked by.
He sat close to the animal and stroked it as it gasped
for air. And today, I remember the twist of his neck,
how he looked into the animal's eyes, like a mother
with a child's fever, waiting for the heat to break.

a quiet room

softly speaking
quietly reading
playing with her dolls alone
on a green carpet
her grassy yard
the white bed covers
with green piping
to match the carpet
I see her there now
her small face looks up
open
and remember walking with her
and in the little boat at the park
buying ice cream
reading the book before bedtime
how do I remember that
how do I recall her dancing
the steps and the movement
and her first boyfriend
and his car
and my worries about
who she will be
how can I remember all that
and remember her now
sitting quietly in the room
reading
as I read
and talking with me
asking me a question of how come
how do I remember
I don't
I forget and listen
for she is remembering now

two flowers

I walked to school with a girl
whose name I cannot recall.
Her blond hair was short
and it curled into her smile.
Each day, we stopped
at her father's flower shop.
Each time I waited with our books
on the ground between my feet.
And when she returned
she always held two flowers,
one for me and one for her.
Her father leaned at the door
and watched as we pinned the
flowers to each other's shirt.
We married each time we stopped there.
And today, I cannot recall her name.
She died when I was too young
to remember death.
One petal lifted from all those flowers
into a New York wind,
and I chased it,
but it flew so high
that it finally disappeared.

wartime or Florence

my cousin wore khaki
he carried his gun
as lightly as a walking stick
touched my head, wordless,
the quieted room spoke of absence
as if a bird had just flown

we crowded into a black car
and drove to the sea
to a ship as large as the building we lived in
it pitched and rolled at heavy ropes
like a Joe Louis fight
the ocean was aroused, uncaring

steam clouded over dim lights
like a party at the end of summer
iron rivets
like many eyes
the rust-stained tears seemed as recent
as the last embrace

men hurried aboard
cars turned on headlights
to light the way
headlights painted black
to hide from invasions,
and I hugged him

my face against the thick wool of his coat
it smelled of just fallen rain
when he climbed aboard
the black car pulled away

its tires, unable to grasp the wet trolley tracks,
slipped, and I felt the ship slide into the sea

when he returned,
he did not speak, nor did I
ask him about the moon
or the mountains
or the snowstorms
where his brother's feet lay frozen

he remained silent
placed his gun
at the door
and walked upstairs.
when he found Florence
he married her

I cannot tell you how long it takes to be a poet

perhaps as long as it takes the sounds of animals
to invade an already inflated tire
and come out again in a slow leak
onto a desolate summer road
or perhaps the time it takes for sewed-on stars
to roll from a silk brocade
hung like the marriage of old people
or to walk among chairs
and touch the light blue tinge of wind
that blows in from an orange-colored sunset
silhouettes of kids on bikes
at the end of a parade

I can tell you
that this amount of time
is all it takes
but I do not know for sure
it may be the grip on my collar
the time it takes to pull it together
to button it
to let it pull at my neck
like a rope
suspended for an ordinary prisoner
or the fan
how it turns
shadows that move like boxers on the ceiling
it is that amount of time, perhaps
lovers as they call each other's names
the birds at daybreak
their chatter a language
unintelligible
to those that hear it
for the first time

or the time it takes seams of dust
to form, to come together
like zippers
held there
like the fastened earth
holds a swamp
or the whistle
of wind
as it plays into the sounds of mountains
loses itself as quickly
as a racer over the line
it is that silence
when it stops
the poem
may be there
that empty bag
wrapped so tightly
to the tree it came from
the cry has no will of its own
the force of wind
topples one more tree
into the sea
to roll over and over
touch the shore
roll back
return
it ends like the last page of a book
quiet
late at night
when all the lights are on

dog dreams

my dog dreams loudly
corners things and cries
climbs trees like a cat
but never goes higher
than her paws
some things we will never do
some things the sky does not touch
she whimpers at the foot of my bed
and I wonder if it is fear
if fear comes with memory
and I wonder if the pictures
from the night on the floor
come at her like a fast train
and I wonder how long it takes for
her to forget a dream
and why dreams are lost in daylight
stories like washed out pages
letters as indecisive moments
lost sentences
lost light
fragments like the remnants of a storm
tree branches
fallen signs from screws
that move like broken arms
and the next night she lies there
on the white tiles near the door
and whimpers and cries again
and I wonder if it's about oscar
the black dog that moved away
the cat who lived in the yard at the old house
and I wonder if memory is like a streamer
in the sky behind a plane
as she goes into sleep

and pictures come by in color
like comic books that float on the sea
and she tries to touch them
as they float on waves close to shore
but cannot reach them because she
does not swim

Vogel's boat

He came upon a pond, and a small wooden boat. Alone in the water, it did not move. It seemed carved from a solid block of wood. Seats, there were two of them. They were carved from the same block. A rope was tied to a tree stump at the side of the pond. Vogel climbed into the small boat. Children were playing on a patch of grass. Mothers sat on a bench and watched the children play. There were no sounds. There was no breeze on the pond. The water did not move. Vogel leaned over the side of the boat to touch the water. Just space. Nothing there. Emptiness in the blue black below the boat. Vogel wondered where he was. He gazed upward at the sky. There were curved wooden rafters, under a tin corrugated roof. He was in a large warehouse. Inside, he thought. The world out there. Large metal roll up door at one end of the warehouse. A projector through a small hole in the ceiling. A shaft of light. The sun. Lights through the ceiling. Like sunshine. Vogel turned again to the children. They stopped playing. Perfectly still. Vogel left the boat, and walked to the children. As he approached, he realized they were images, projected. He looked up, the light of the projector was off. He walked to the women on the bench. They stopped talking as Vogel approached. Again, they were there, projected. Vogel turned back to the boat. He touched the wood. Nothing. It too was an image from a hole in the ceiling. He sat again, in the boat. And the lights dimmed. Vogel was the first to disappear. His projection went out quickly.

Vogel is a character our father created. Perhaps he was our father's alter ego.

conversation with Rose

goodbye rose
goodbye murray

they killed me murray

I know rose

they wanted my jewelry
and took my glasses
I couldn't see when
they choked me
it didn't take long
to kill me

I know rose
it's like the day our father died
and then mother
a month later
and now you
I feel so bad
all over again

I'm sorry murray

it's not your fault
rose
they killed you

did you like your life rose?

yes and no murray
there were good things
and there were problems too

the road

I lose so many poems as I drive
that I write on a cardboard box
on the steering wheel
with the seat belt on.
The belt gives me a sense
of safety as I drive and write.
It is hard to remember words
that mean something to others.
I hold back in conversations
with people close to me.
I do not want them to know
about my breath in the morning,
or how I feel about getting older.
Perhaps they won't stay
and finish the ride.

kiss

Yesterday, the poems
came later
as I drove the car
on a beautiful day.
I pulled over
to write
on the steering wheel
at a red light.
Like the woman
who combed her hair,
put lipstick on,
sucked her lips,
to smooth the color
and threw me a kiss
as I watched.

no vacancy

I drive past the Pavilion Motel on Pico
a young boy with no shirt
and cutoff jeans
sits on a low stucco wall
his right leg extends
like a bow
and he sunbathes as this traffic
goes by
and I think of my son
when he was young
and wonder what he thought as I passed him
in those days
what boys think of
as I pass this kid

and I wonder if it is always
the same
how each childhood and adulthood
bridge these years
and how boredom mixes with the
restless urge of where and what
and I wonder if my son knows
what this boy is thinking
if even my son is too old now
to remember
and I wonder if it's about
places these cars come from
or where they go
these men who drive by
who were boys who sat on walls like him
and thought
about being older
and how sex worked

and how their next day would soon
fall from a familiar neighborhood
and the surrender of family
how all those years
of sleeping late,
would lead them to hard work and
boredom again
to loss
and how loss suffers least when it expends itself
like a passing car
how each car seems to know
and how each of us
returns by always turning right,
again and again
and how we forget the past,
and that light, it turns green now
and reminds me to move on
before it is over.

credence

Eight o'clock in the morning. I can hear
the ocean outside the window. I follow
the waves like a shade rolling to the floor,
up again, and down, over and over.
And I sit and write. She sits next to me
and reads a script. Words about people,
and people with words. And I think about
the scale I want to buy. I wonder how
accurate it is. The old scale weighs about
three pounds less than an accurate one.
I feel good on that scale, but it is old
and streaked with so many dried showers.
A new one would look better, but I just
don't trust that it will tell the truth.

25¢ pin

My mother didn't hug me
when
she was young.
When
we were older
I hugged her
and remembered
her birthday
as I did as a young boy,
when I bought her a pin
at Woolworths for
25 cents.
The first present I bought
for a woman.
It was in the shape of a rose
with glitter stones
like diamonds
and a hollow back
with brushed-on gold paint.
She acted surprised
and told me she loved it.
And wore it on a black dress
with padded shoulders.
And after that
I do not remember
seeing her wear it
again.
Later,
I came across it in her drawer
and didn't care that
she never wore it.
That she only wore

my father's jewelry.
I was happy I bought it
for her.
And I never gave it a thought,
until now.

conversation with Dad

(by Donna Marlene Josephs)

So, Dad, you're not here anymore.

No, I'm not, Donna. I'm Here.

Where?

In a place that is hard to describe.

Are you okay, Dad?

Yeah. I'm doing great!
No more pain, no more suffering.
I'm in Nana's kitchen
reading the newspaper and sipping coffee.

How are Nana and Grandpa?

They are wonderful, young!
You should see them.

Are you lonely, Dad?

Are you kidding?
There is so much love here,
that loneliness has no place.

Did you meet the little girl
with the blonde hair that curled
into her smile?

Oh, yes. She's here.

She's a woman now.
She is full of love, and she goes to earth to help people.
They'll be training me soon.
I'll be down on earth to help others.
I'm looking forward to it.

Will you help us, Dad?

Absolutely. I already am.
I'll send you good advice when you need it.

Thank you, Dad.
Ira and I really appreciate your love.
We miss you. So does Cody.

You're welcome, Baby. I love you.
Call on me whenever you want.
I'm right here with you.

What are you gonna' do today?

I'm going to the museum with the woman who
has the blonde hair that curls into her smile.
We'll pin flowers on each other's shirts –
like the old times.

That sounds nice. Have fun, Papa Bear.
I love you.

I love you too, Honey.

children's stories

she wants to know why I write poetry
who for
and why not children's
stories
about people made of names
and bright ideas
picture books

and I try to explain about poetry
how the compressed
sounds
are the rhythm
the drums
the tap under
a bass fiddle
how it is not even the words

but the suddenness
of a man at the door
with iron limbs
that begin to harden
because he hesitates
to run
like tap water
to clear himself
to remove the rust
before it forms
but knows he cannot
until he is ready
to say it in a poem

proof

Science has no way of knowing the
consequences of behavior, the nuances,
the faults, the undiscovered quilts
in the brain.
The birds, the trees, the mornings,
the evenings.
It is all in the bible, but science
is the discontent child.
The bible uses premises
that have hair on them,
that tuck into the dark,
that ignite, and call out,
and grope like fish in the
sea.

Science has no errors, but its
own faulty steps
that have to be proven,
or the mountain falls,
that have to be proven,
or the rain flies instead of the birds
that have to proven,
or the fish walk
that have to be proven, or
man deceives himself
into a new
way to the top of a hill.
Science has no way of proving
itself in a dream, or even in the
newest bible.
The new one is written like
a story and the
story is incomplete

like all stories.
I told my kids stories,
stories about alligators
and how a coconut
fell from a tree and
knocked out the alligator.
Beaned it like a baseball hits
an unaware umpire.
They laughed
because I couldn't prove it,
and wanted more, but I
told them about gravity
and the sense it all made
and they fell asleep
and only remembered the story.

the assault

(by Donna Marlene Josephs)

A poem strikes
uninvited.
I fumble in my purse
a pen
the back of a business card.
The steering wheel
is my table.
I think of Dad
how he fumbled
for a pen
a piece of cardboard
and how he used
this table
in this car
to relieve his soul
from the poems
that burned within.

P.S. 51

alphabet
over the blackboard
some letters I knew
and others were tough
how many of you can recite
the alphabet
did not raise my hand
the principal shaped like a bell
called my mother
waited in the empty room
with Rochelle
she wore a pink dress
black hair
curls lay against her head
like a slinky
alert
waiting for the contest
my mother arrived
Rochelle read from a book
that's the way to read
your son cannot
mother looked at those curls
bewildered
her accent dulled
when she said let's go
we left that room
walked
not talking
we stopped for herring
he climbed the ladder
looking back over his shoulder

smiling at mother and me
wrapped it in white paper
then with newspaper
the same newspaper mother could not read
we held hands and walked home

stories or P.S. 51 continued

When I was older, I learned about clouds, and how geography
was put on a map, and made of dirt.
And I learned to read, but remembered the girl.
And never forgot her name.
And the Principal, and how she didn't smile.
And now I read, and write, and swing by that school
in Richmond Hill, and wonder how small it must be, that
it couldn't house a place other than classrooms.
A room for kindness, where you reach in and come out
with a crystal that lights up every time
you approach yourself for love.

go between

I love mom
but don't tell her

dad's supposed to
but he tells me

he worries to me
she's gotten old

broods about her without him
if he dies

he worries his love quietly
and tells me but not her

she knows
but is silent

she sits quietly
and sleeps

the fight

tightened lips
over words
grip the door
dulled explosion
she leaves the car
tears hidden
from me
walking alone
into the crowd
an alien
in a city of arrivals
disappears
I am alone at the window
father stares
he drives home without her
later, she returns quietly
and learns to stay
do not get angry
you'll get sick
you are a young father
you can learn to be kind
like I am to you
your father works hard
speaks harshly
you can learn to look away
swallow your courage
look for an excuse
always find a way
do not get angry
you'll get sick
eat, then you can play

under smiles

I've never seen him angry
he's that kind of man.
Even when he is angry,
his face doesn't show it.
Other men I've known
are the same way.
Their faces, and how they smile
when angry.
Not the sarcastic smile
of hate
or the violent crime
under that smile.
They truly are kind
and have no fight,
but the butcher paper
they are wrapped in.

kindness

I read a story today
About a crazed hyena
And how it took chunks
Of the arm and leg
Of a woman
Who loves animals.
How the boundary
Crossed
Between that woman
And the animal.
How the violence of
The hyena
Became a reality
And how the amazed
Face of the woman
Shrieked at the
Animal's kindness
When it let her live.

danger or exposure

I have to leave soon,
and go to work.
There is so much
to write about.
A lifetime of exposure.
Like that guy
whose eyes were black,
and darting, and marble like.
He walked around and
around the examination
room. He threatened
to break the door.
The nurses asked me
to call the cops.
But I went in there
and stared into the black
of his eyes
and told him
I cared about him
until he cried.

Angelo

I hung out at the register before customers arrived,
leaned against the cash drawer and watched Angelo.
He bent over the opened box of plums,
one arm behind to balance himself,
as if he were ready to do a somersault,
graceful, his long body leaned into the window
to place the plums in rows like summer grass,
each row meticulous
he turned toward me
held a plum far above his head
turned it slowly in wrinkled fingers
that seemed like small ladders.
"These are fine looking kelseys," he said to me,
but kept looking at the plum like a lover,
whispered words
kept turning the green plum lightly
as if it were a beach ball.
A loud voice intruded as my father appeared below him,
looked into Angelo's eyes with scorn.
"Those plums are green gage,"
and stood back triumphantly to watch the tall man
collapse into himself, his head turned back into the light
like a cornered animal in the night,
and ground into his false
teeth with murmurs of Italian curses
quickly turned back into that window
continued to lean far over into the rows of green plums
to find the perfect curve, and when he found it,
let it settle into tissue paper crushed under each one,
like his heart held a cigarette between his lips,
his eyes closed to the sting of the smoke,
but father returned to the window, not yet content,
looked up at Angelo, as if he were standing below a tall tree.

"They're green gage," he said again, and turned toward me,
shook his head, squeezed his eyes in mockery.
Angelo turned away, walked behind my father
to wait on the first customer,
and marked the small paper bag with a crayon
drawn from behind his ear and heard him say to the woman
that the plums were kelseys,
and spoke quietly of the reasoning
I could not hear
my father hated Angelo ever since he called the union
and complained that he was asked to carry
heavy cases of soda from the basement.
My father resented him more, when he said he was
a fruit and vegetable man,
not a laborer
he got back at Angelo each year when those green plums arrived,
attacked his knowledge,
but Angelo knew it was because of the old resentment,
and they battled each year,
each one with seething anger
whenever those green plums arrived
from the market
in the dark hours before dawn,
in the summer in the store
where I watched men do battle over plums,
not willing to say what hurt them
or what pain they inflicted on each other
each one,
each year,
the dance,
unresolved till this day
I still do not know the name of those damn plums

looking for God

I saw Leo today.
His eyes were puffy
and he squeezed them shut
like the other times
he imparted a truth
that he and I both understood.
Like the time he spoke of love,
how he loved the Polish girl.
How she made him feel,
and how that love carried him
through the war.
I asked him about the high holidays,
if he had gone to the synagogue,
and he told me that he did go,
but showed me a silver crucifix
that he carried in his pocket
when he went to pray.
"I take it with me,
because I don't know
who to pray to.
The same cross
placed on my neck,
by a friend, as I lined up
to be marched away
as a Jew."
And he squeezed his eyes
as he told me the story,
while his fingers writhed in his pocket
as he searched for God again,
as he looked down,
not wanting to be seen.

leeches

I've wanted love before. Thought I had it. But until now I don't think I did. It's new. I know that. But it seems real. I never trusted love. It seemed alien. I always had to prove something. I equated anger with loss. Gone away. Love is staying. Hanging in. Not leaving. Knowing it's the long haul. I know it with her. Don't trust it yet. Like the loft. Don't trust sleeping up there. Seems alien. The room has a vaulted ceiling, like the apex of a Church. And lights I cannot reach. They shine into the center, onto the computer, like floodlights at a supermarket opening. I close the doors to that room when it rains. Water seeps under the door and begins to warp it, shape the fibers a different way. Like pregnancy. A new beginning. Irregular and dark. And the ground sponged with flowers. You can tell I'm not morbid today. But I feel guilty not seeing my Dad. It's a holiday, and I haven't seen him yet. But I know he's okay, and I can't replace my Mother. I guess that's what I am. My Mother. I've always been her. Listening to him. Loving him in spite of his harshness. Forgiving. Looking for an excuse. Embarrased about myself. And I have a slight murmur. A slap in my heart. That's what the doctor said. Take antibiotics when you go to the dentist, just to make sure. How can I make sure about death? How can I arrange not doing it? When all there is, is death at the end. Which actually feels celebratory this morning. Just a part of life, as long as I don't get into the missing, and the self pity. We all have to do it. Like diving into unknown water, where the leeches are. I came out of that water as fast as I went in. Didn't want a leech on me. Didn't want to find a black squirmy piece of jell on me, somewhere on my leg, and have to pull it off and quickly throw it into lye. The silver kerosene can at the side of the lake. Shiny, but spotted and the label peeled off. The leech sizzled in there. Turned white, like a fire, late at night, near the end. Occasional small eyes of orange. I swam quickly to escape them. Not like the kids who stayed in long and didn't care. Didn't care about the leech , and how it started to stick into the skin, like a straw in a malted, and begin to suck. I ran quickly each time. Dove in, and ran out. Quickly checked my arms and legs and torso. And more than once, felt something on my back, like a long fingernail begin to dig in. But it was my imagination. Like death. Like death is the beginning again. There is no arranging it. It comes like a train. Quickly in the night, and then gone. Like my Mother. Her valve closed up. Quickly. She went quickly. Shook her head when they mentioned surgery, and wonder if my valve will close like hers, and the pain of everyone who knows me, around the bed. And I wonder if I could just dive in quickly, and come back, not stay long enough for a leech to attach. And walk away to a cool tent, and lie on the cot with a comic book. I'd just lay there, and watch that can sizzle.

lost

Last night the printer disappeared
when I clicked the print icon
I waited and was informed
that it could not be found
I looked down at the low
red table where the printer
sits, and sure enough it was
there feeling lonely and lost

the king

this morning
I turn to walk away
and notice a snail on an empty wine bottle
made of white glass
flat
the bottle of a street person
tossed there to be forgotten
thrown under the bush
at the side of the gate
and when I return
it is still there
and when I see the snail again
I see him as a king
from the past
as he tries to eat the bottle
but cannot chew a hole in its hardness
and stays there overnight
and in the morning
I look for him
and see him
on the label now
as he attempts to chew the paper
but the glue is strong
and the bottle holds it
as if it were a blanket on a cold
night
and only room for one
and after another night on the bottle
the snail trails away
leaves a line on the cement
and turns back once
as it remembers
how hard it is to be a king

on ironing his own shirt

he told me there was something spiritual
about ironing his own shirt
as we talked on the phone
he wore a headset that made him
mobile in his room
an ironing board in front of him
his right arm locked into extension
as he guided the iron around the
buttons, erasing the creases
at the edge of the shirt
then the collar
and the cuffs
and as he ironed
his right biceps
flickered and chewed
as if eating

he spoke of arrival at a new
place
about coming into light
from darkness
and how prayer helped him
to stand at his own table
to smooth his own
shirt
and when he was finished
he selected the hanger
to hold his new whiteness
against the sky
of his room

and his arms rested

as if he were the Lord
on the seventh day
as he sat back on the couch
the shirt calm and powerful
waited for his arms
the iron upright
on the board
and at that moment
I wondered about the path
it took for a man to come to this
pause that his ironing board
became the final rock
to climb for him to reach
the other side

Joe's funeral

I feel like someone died this morning.
After a fight, I feel as if a death occurs.
The phone rang.
It was my cousin to tell me
that her husband died.
His name was Joe.
And she wants me to come to the funeral,
but I keep on thinking about the fight,
how we talk to each other,
how feelings get hurt by the ones
we love.
And she says she doesn't get it.
That it's an age thing.
That maybe I'm older,
that I want too much respect.
And why bother with respect.
At her age the coffin stays open
longer, and you can party at
the funeral.
And now Joe's dead,
and his family wants me to come
to pay my respects,
and I'm not in the mood
after all this arguing,
to deal with his death.
But they beg me on the phone,
they expect me,
I'm their only family, they say,
and I owe it to Joe who was a good man.
And I decide to go,
and he doesn't even know
that I may show up at his funeral
with my feelings hurt.

rehearsal

an old man on an open patio
spots of sun on his face
like fish in clear water
tosses breadcrumbs to the
pigeons that
circle his feet
like a carousel
and when there is no more bread
he falls asleep between two trees

I sit on the same patio with my father
who points to his tomato plant
near the old man
"it is in the pot with the evergreen tree
it will grow tomatoes
like the ones we grew before I came here
before your mother died
before we left the garden we loved"
and when he tells me about my mother
he kisses his fingers
"she was so delicious
and that pot of soil over there
is the only earth left to me"
and then he too slumps and sleeps

and the pigeons lift from the feet of the old man
a squadron into the sky
by tall buildings
and wonder
how long
before I am old
before I am here
before the final flight

before I sleep
as they do
as the pigeons flutter
as they fly away
as they disappear
at the end of each day

the way a doctor looks

did you ever know a guy like me
who didn't look like a doctor
a guy that looked like a native
an indian
or an innkeeper
a watch repairman
or a man of the sea
did you
did you ever know a man who looked like a doctor
gray hair at the temples, a nose slightly turned at the tip
to hold his glasses
now that guy looks like a doctor
and I was near him
said yes, you look like a doctor
so I became one
and now that woman says, you don't look like a doctor
who am I then
I am there with gray at the temple, an upturned nose, and
my glasses at the tip
dismayed by her surprise
I am in there looking out into a room of men in white coats
leaning into a silver vat, where bodies float
shriveled corpses, tags on their ankles
we fish for one, the formaldehyde as pungent as rotten
limburger cheese in my father's car the night I took out a girl
and stopped the car looking for the dog shit I knew I stepped in
we placed the body on the steel table and studied the ways of the
arteries and nerves, the corpse kept alive for that semester
preserved each night in that vat
and now she asks again
somehow you don't look like a doctor
and I carve at the corpse
again and again

Vogel and the bullet

Vogel knew he was being watched. Why would he stand there with a newspaper. His heart raced. His chest began to ache. If he had only taken the other road. Damn. He turned away. Sat at the table. The cafe was empty. A small man, bald, with scorching silvery eyes, approached the table wearing a white apron tied at the waist. He held a pad in front of his chin. Looking straight ahead, he asked Vogel what he could get for him. Coffee. Just coffee for now. The waiter left. A coin arose on the table. It looked like a quarter. But it was a flattened bullet. Vogel knew his time was short. He dropped to the floor as the burst of fire began. The shots were loud as they came across the cafe. The waiter returned as if nothing happened. The coffee was hot. Vogel lay under the table and asked if he could have the coffee down there. Vogel paid with the flattened coin. The waiter reshaped the coin into a small bullet. Placed it in his teeth and raised his hands. He walked out into the plaza and paraded the caught bullet in his teeth. His friends were amazed. Vogel rose, drank the coffee, and left the square unnoticed.

Krausman's Colonial House

my mother stood on the green lawn
white chairs were slung low under a large tree,
her long blond hair fell like the river onto white shoes
concealed by the tall grass of summer

I ran from the woods
where I went with father to pick berries
in there, in the absence of sun
on a dark path of vines overgrown by a hundred years.
I became terrified of a snake as it slid under fallen leaves

each step I took, I feared that snake
until I could not go on,
and pulled myself free from those sharp pointy vines
each small cluster, like many shadowed eyes,
and retreated to the sun where I could hear father's laughter
coming from that dark place in the woods

and when I held mother's hand and walked to the brook
I did not tell her of the snake, or the fear of that snake
but that I wished to swim over river rock
to walk on stones that quivered under cold mountain water
and as I swam there, in that pool, another snake slipped by,
quietly
its skin as black as the floor of that forest I just left

and quickly I swam to the edge of that brook, to climb
from that fear again,
but father returned with the berries
and laughingly told her of the snake and my flight from the forest

I dove back into the brook

swam deeply into a forest of drowned grass, no longer clear
where a black night, spiteful, covered the light of the moon
and I slipped quietly, like the serpent, it was silent
and the water was bewildered.

boys

Four boys
in the back seat of an old car.
Two play the guitar,
one sings, and the other hums.
The two remaining boys
shake their heads to the beat.
The car sits on blocks, no wheels.
There is dust under the car
darkened by the shadow of
the sun as it passes overhead
and brightens everything,
except the underneath
the part hidden
the secrets
the deepest part
in there under the car
the song.
The deep penetrating lullaby
forgotten by a mother
and the son
who crawls
into the back seat
as if he were about to remember.

the last party

Hey who's the party for?
We waited in line to get
to the food.
And this kid walks up to me
and asks me who's the party for.
And I told him it was for his
grandfather, that his grandfather
died and left the earth
and the party was to celebrate
his life.
And he told me he had been
told that his grandfather died
by his mother, but she forgot
to tell him who the party was for.
And when I told him, he seemed
puzzled. Didn't quite get it.
Didn't quite know what to make
of a party where the guest of honor
wasn't there. And he thought about it
and pictured his grandfather
halfway out of the earth
eating cake.

goodbyes....

(by Donna Marlene Josephs)

Goodbyes are so
hard.
Perhaps our experiences
are like the
gray ribbons of
smoke —
from the Shabbat candles
floating, dancing in
swirls and curls
until they disappear into the air.
Do experiences puff away like that?
Or do they rest
as fertile seeds in
the soil of our hearts
growing vines of love
and memories that
we take with us
wherever we go....

the big one

I invited everyone who passed by.
Mother was upstairs wondering where they all came from.
I don't feel like that party now.
And I don't care about the gifts.
I'd rather hike, or go to the beach.
I'd rather be with her.
Tell some guys about the birthday. Let them buy me coffee
and let it go.
Like a paper sailboat. Light and easy.
Watch it float on a pond in Queens.
The one I jumped into on a cold fall day,
dressed up for aunt Rose.
New clothes. And now I was soaked.
She said I had to go in the old ones, and I didn't care.
I didn't want to be that sterile.
I wanted to be loose, like the grass in a mower.
And now it's the same.
I want to dance to the sounds of a full orchestra.
"I'd like to be in America." That's the kind of song.
The song I hear when I have nothing to do.
The beat of wrapping paper in an afternoon wind.
I'd like to sail through this birthday like a boat on a large lake.
Quietly. Far out, where you can hardly see me.
I'd like to step on broken bottles,
and not worry about getting cut.
I'd like to walk with my dog as if we had just left the century.
Pour vinegar over fish and chips.
Come out from under a bridge in London and step into a taxi.
Return to Claridges, and take a long hot bath.
Put on a robe so thick, it feels like the soft nails of a lover.
I'd like to walk on rose petals, the rust colored ones that float
to the floor, and lie there like the softness of my dog's ears.
I'd like to press my face onto a cold window in San Francisco,

and watch the rain splatter.
See a reflection of her as she steps from the shower,
her hair like a wet blush.
Watch her shake her head,
and place the cup of cappuccino to her lips.
I'd like to rest in her arms, her legs draped over me like a flag.
I'd like to walk away from a hotel with the largest umbrella
and see the Sun begin to slowly emerge as if I was the World
and the Sun were coming up for me.
I'd like this birthday to move on
like the last train out of a station.
I'd like to stand for a moment on the platform,
and listen to the wheels fade into silence.
It would be enough.

post-op

my crutch leans on the brown
coffee table
the unruly planks of carved trees
my foot lies on it
fears the night
as the pain begins again
throbs like a cherry in my mouth
and I threaten to swallow the pit
my Father's voice is low on the phone
I hear him behind a trumpet
on the radio.
he is depressed.
I tell him I had an operation on my big toe.
"So I guess I'm not going to see you tomorrow,"
and doesn't ask me about my pain.
He is too old, and hurts more than my toe
"You won't see me," I tell him. "Not tomorrow
but when I feel better."

there is still time
after the pain
I can recover
but not him
and the blues play
the piano and the
trumpet
and I cry
when he talks to me
in that gray tone of faded sweaters
the marbled breath of hopeless loss
hit and miss rhythm on the radio,
and I want to call him back,
to hear him chant this music

with me, at a honky tonk bar
at another bus stop
but now
it is before morning
hours away
and it is so late

naked

I walk
naked
and alone
except
for the dog
and I think about the old lady who lived
here before me
who was taken away
after she walked naked
and became senile
and was put into a home
and I think about
her eyes
how they must have
looked back
inside of her
as they took her
from this house
by the sea
and years later
I too walk as she did
not as old
and not senile
but settled in
like the dew
how it knows
where to be each morning
how night after night
rain runs onto billboards
and washes colors
into themselves
as if they were all the same
and as she leaves

I offer her a sweatshirt
to keep her warm
in case she gets the urge
to dance naked
one more time

Vogel singing

Vogel entered the room. Walked into the choir, and began to sing as loud and as clear as he could. The master approached him from behind. Leaned in to hear Vogel sing. He stood back, after a moment, and said, you are not singing, young man. You make no sound. But I am dear master. I gave it all I had. I sang loud and clear. The clearest I have ever sung. Well, he said, let me hear you alone. He raised his hand to silence the choir. And Vogel sang. With eloquence, and fine-formed sounds, like a bird. See, you mouth the words, but we do not hear. The choir looked at Vogel, amazed at the beauty of his voice. The master asked the choir to sing again. They sang, but Vogel only saw their mouths move this time. Not a sound. He understood. He asked the master if he could sing again. If the sounds were not there, what matter. The master agreed, and Vogel sang again. This time the master heard the singing. The beauty was too much. He asked him to stop. Vogel returned to the forest, where he continued to sing. The birds heard him, and flew to his tree. The master turned back to the choir. What a shame I cannot hear his voice.

swimmer

the old man
enters slowly
unsteady
on the bold rocks
he waits
in the cold
green water
as it rises to his thighs
then to his buttocks
a wave rolls
pulling him upward
he vaults over
into the sea
on his back
arms rotating
up and over
paddling like
a river boat

waiting to play

There was a dog on the beach this morning
He carried a red ball the size of a soccer ball
It had teeth marks scarred into its density
He dropped the ball at my feet
Waited for me to pick it up
To throw it for him to retrieve
I had just awakened and was about
To walk my dog
I did not want to play
It was too early I thought
And I left him there
In front of the red ball on a gray morning
The only color on the beach
And I wonder if the color I see
Is the same color animals see
If red is truly red to a dog
Or just a ball
And how I would know
And I wondered if we danced
Would the animals know we are dancing
Or would they just see us move to music
And wait for us to stop or would
They remember some other time
When they were more than animals
When dance was as important as fire
And how they would gather in a circle
On a summer evening look up at the
Stars and howl and how after announcing
Their presence they would move
Rhythmically each one increasing the
Cadence as the music drummed
and how each one knew how

to step to the beat the circle turning
faster now one dog pulls into the
middle and kicks his legs in the air
his front paws on the ground as if
a gymnast and then the others
one by one performing as if they were
at a wedding giving away the bride and groom
singing to the air and summer flies
a fire behind them the moon overhead
curling into darkness by a cloud
and when the fire light dims one dog howls
again and they trail off
with one dog who stands alone in the darkness
a red ball on the ground waiting for me to play.

full circle

There are two reasons I stay sane.
One, is that old dirt
in corners of rooms
will always be there
no matter
how hard I try to clean.
The other,
is the dancing bear.
The dancing bear, and the music.
And how a bear can go from
one foot to the other and stay stable.
Like the first date, and the preparation.
For these two reasons
– dirt and bears that dance –
I stay sane
because there is no other way.

mother's grocery list

I think about things
And weigh each word as if I were
A clerk in a fruit and vegetable store,
Like my father, with a cigarette in his mouth,
And his long arms rising out of
A soiled apron,
His fingers are thick
As they hold the brown paper
Bag and the fruit he selects.

"Just one pound, you said," and
Places the bag, just aired open with
A snap of his elbow, onto the pan
Of the scale, a silver dish
Suspended over rows of fruit.
And as he wrinkles closed the sack of
Plums, or perhaps they were cherries,
"I never make money on cherries," he says,
"You guys sample too many," as he
Smiles and looks at me, as he hands
The fruit to a customer.

And my mother's call at the end
Of the day, to tell me what to bring
Home. And if she didn't call, I'd have to
Call her. She waited for the call when
Her list was not composed. And I'd
Have to be patient as she thought
About things, as I waited for the next
Item, "And oh yes, I need milk,
And maybe napkins." And she would scratch
Her head at this point, squint
Her eyes, knowing there was something

She forgot. "Anything else?" I'd say.
"No, that's it."

And when we came home, my father carried
The box of groceries on his shoulder, his
Opposite hand balanced it behind
His head, as he held on to the opened top of the
Cardboard, a bunch of celery upright as if
It was a telescope. And when he placed
It on the kitchen table, she would
Look in there, push things around,
Frown, and say, "You forgot the tomatoes."
My father would raise his eyes, and turn to me,
And throw his hands in the air as if he were a
Minstrel on a stage, and say, "The woman didn't
Tell you to bring tomatoes, did she?"

At that point she positioned her hands
On her hips and scowled as if she just
Tasted sour milk. "Of course I told you
Tomatoes."
And me, on the side, I tried
To settle the issue as the order taker,
The one who knew, but at that point
It wasn't about truth. And after a while,
My mother, so sure about the tomatoes,
I had to confess,
"We must have forgotten."

And now vindicated, "See Murray,
Even Stanley knows the truth."
And me, as she turns away,
I raise my hands to my father,
Like he did, and
Lift my shoulders,

Into a what's-one-to-do pose.
She was sure of it, and it wasn't worth
Fighting over. We were tired,
And laughed, and she smiled,
As we went on to eat the
Steak or lamb chops,
Or if it was Thursday, it would be
Salmon salad, or broiled fish that
Was smelly and dry,
And there was no lemon.

Because she forgot to tell us
About the fish and didn't remember
The lemons. And we struggled
Through another meal,
The remembrance of
Things a bit hazy now,
Like her list,
Always missing something
We forgot to bring.

midnight

a quiet voice

sounds

too loud

late

at night

hungry

for silence

revolution

all night
the rain falls
heavy as milk
against these windows
in the hospital where my father's
cheeks sink
into his face
his eyes are open
as he reaches for my hand
the grip is weak
like the slowing of the rain
and my face is the wetness of the water
as it trails off
as I remember his power
when the rain struck hard against the house
when he got up to go to the market,
to go to work, in a storm
and how he lies in bed now
with swollen feet
and a Polish nurse who calls him "baby" and "love"
and turns him, and bathes him, and holds him,
and a guitar-playing Elvis impression
is all I hear
and she tells me she came to visit
and never returned to Poland
her face is wide at the top
and narrow at the bottom
like a shield
large glasses over darting black eyes
"he tries so hard,
and you can't leave him,
he wants to be touched."
she goes on to tell me

she came here
with her daughter,
and stayed because the revolution started in Poland
and that she will never return
and tells me she only eats vegetables
the size of apples
and the core remains in her hair
and she continues to talk
as she returns to my father
to help him turn
as he turned from Europe
when he ran from his revolution
from the cold feet of rain
and now she turns him
and whispers "easy baby, easy my love,"
the sound that remains
like the blades of a windmill
during each revolution

running out of ink

there are other pens
but I stick to this one
and continue to run out of ink
less and less
and I fear this running out
this disappearing
this darkness
that becomes lighter as I write
less visible
like an old note to myself
pinned on a water damaged door
faded
all becomes fainter
memories
faces
and now that they fade
I miss them
and want them
and when they were here
I found their bold strokes
dark colors
too strong
too deep
like the largest lake
the colors of blue black
how that strength scares me
and how I miss it
and want the flow of sounds
on paper
and now I want faces I once had
and now fear

I am losing
because the pen slowly runs dry
and I press harder
but soon before I discard it
I will have forgotten why
I started

not my dog

I think my dog is the unabomber
she hides her chemistry set in the
quiet recesses of the house.
I know it's here.
And down the hallway, I see
her head between front paws.
She looks innocent as she waits for
me to leave, to get to the
experiments.
Her mixtures of fertilizer and
sour pickles ground into the
quisinart, and boiled into a viscous
solution to look like balsamic vinegar.
All this to throw me off,
bottles like salad dressing.

She thinks about shock, and where
she'll strike next.
I know how innocent she looks.
Her gray eyebrows, those white
paws, the coat of black hair that
sheds so easily in my car.
But she ships out letter
bombs. I know it. Who else but
her lonely mind when I'm gone.
The warped way of seeing.
The anger and frustration of not
hunting anymore. Of sitting in boredom
as the maid shoos her with a broom.
And all the time the terror of a bomb.
And how she chooses.
How she thinks of a letter, and gives

it form, and when it becomes, let's say
a W, she fixes on an occupation
that starts with W, like a warehouseman,
then thinks of a warehouse, full of
TV's. Then a leader in the field.
Someone who failed
to recognize Vietnam as a fiasco.
Then thinks of a holiday symbol,
a christmas tree, a bulb, and decides it
will be a gift of a christmas tree bulb.
And with that she picks a man who
said something so many years ago,
and soon forgot.
And she puts the liquid with the charge,
and winds the tape.
All this while I'm at work, and hides it
until the mailman comes, and slips him the
package, and returns to the steps
at the window where she watches
the street. Innocent, and helpless
as she sighs when I return.

But I know and do not speak up,
to tell the story, to upset the case
against Koczyinski, and she paws me,
to throw me off again, begs for
a cookie, and I give in, and wonder
who's next, and how long will
I hide this dog,
knowing what I know.

Jacque

Jacque rides his bicycle
onto the boardwalk
as he has done
so many times before.
I hear the squeak of his wheels,
how his cadence slows.
He rides the same faded red bicycle,
no gears, old and rusty.
He swims each day.
Today the sea is prepared, the wind
whips at the waves, under a sun
that is farther out.
I notice the sudden leap into age.
How the skin of his face drapes
and maps the shape of his skull,
like I've seen in other old men.
The ones that sat on chairs with my father
before he died.
Jacque has always looked fit,
a small black bathing suit
on a young man's torso.
But today, in this subdued light
I see his leathery skin
stretched onto dried bone
like the grayed skull
of a desert horse,
left in the sand and sun
so many years before
without a bicycle
to ride home on.

vows

I asked her if they still fight.
"After thirty years
there is nothing
left to fight about.
We've had so many fights,
we fought about everything."
And when she told me that,
I wondered what those fights
were about.
Maps, and where to turn,
or about dogs and smiles,
or perhaps teeth
unblemished by chocolate cake.
And today, still,
I do not know
what they
fought about.
Perhaps it was a dance,
and who should lead
and when the music stops
who smiles first.

dynamite

I receive a phone call from the man
who buries my Father in Israel.
He says, "God should be merciful," after we talk
about the bombing
in Tel Aviv. On the same day my Father is buried.
His casket in the cargo of a plane from New York.
The blast occurs at the time he arrives.
A pedestrian with explosives like a belt,
agitates the ground, as if it were a dance floor filled with students.
And I wonder if my Father can rest under this turbulence,
or will he continue to hear the rumble of bombs
and how it falls and explodes on his ground,
and how that blast pulls at seams of flesh.
How the haunted sound of sirens,
cough like my Father, before he dies.
And whether this last trip is truly worth it.
Whether this dynamite, and how it spreads like earthquakes,
can ultimately bring about the charms of gypsies,
or will this ground be like all the rest,
thoughts of peace like one thick cloud,
how it drops and dusts of air,
how it swallows, rives the earth that covers him
that sound as quiet now
as the lion after eating his prey,
content to lie on cold stones,
like my Father,
so far from America
so far from quiet
so far from peace.

goalie

Today I sit in a chair and look out the window at the fence that separates my yard from the driveway on the other side. Yesterday, I drove into the parking lot at work, and as I turned into the section I park in, the attendant, in his chair, pulled his feet back, twisted his body as if he were a goalie on a hockey team. He sits there to make sure only certain people park in that section. He sits on a folding chair, but the cars, as they make the turn, aim for him as they turn, and he never knows if they will make it. Kind of dangerous to sit there. He'd be better off on skates, so he could skate away at those moments. And now each day that I drive in, I worry that I scare him. Worry that he feels my car is coming after him. Ready to hit him, and knock him over, out of that chair, and I see him wave his arms, turn his legs to the side, like I do at a movie, to let someone walk by, and then sit back in the dark, and wait for the action to start again.

young girl

a young girl screams at a crashing wave
as if she were about to ward off an attack
an exploitation in cold water
and the turtle returns to the sea
slithers in the shadow of night
for it does not elope with the sea
just carries itself silently on a wave

my father's breath

is the fever I turn from
old and stale
it leaves in the night, in his truck
nor does it dress for work in the morning

it calls me on the phone
the breath as shallow as the saucer
it is the breath in his market before dawn
behind the cigarette that dangles from his lips
over boxes of strawberries

it breathes by day
in his store
where it asks me to sweep at dust
and tells me
— if you do a good job, I'll let you do it again
and it is in his song
— there was a boy who ate a lot of stroy
and cried oh boy oh boy oh boy

a scathing breath
— you and me, we're finished
silence from that breath
a silence as shunned as the impact of a plane crash
wraps me in its arms
constricts
until I say,— OK, I'll go to your school

breath on the mirror
clouds after a shower
in there I see my face
his breath
filmy droplets

swirl into an abyss
less than the breath of a small bird

rare old stamps fold in an attic
my father's breath is a shroud
— there was a boy who ate a lot of stroy
I sing to it
and watch him laugh
— your breath is now, I say
— yes, my breath is now

old boots

my father's death
is a kite
floats
and stays high
like the sun
and when it comes down
tomorrow
it is next to my mother
as they are buried together
sunken marble tables
fashioned
of old boots
and shoe laces
and tomorrow
is the day
that is so still
and not yet here

endings

I think about how to
end this poem as I begin,
I think about
the end of a good book.
How two lovers ride
a boat up and down
a river in *Love in the
Time of Cholera.*
She waited a long time
for that love
and so did he.
He did it quietly
and patiently.
Love came to him
in spite of all those years,
and when love came,
it was the end.

photographing Philip Levine

I'd like to photograph Philip Levine
in black and white,
and blow him up
like a billboard on Sunset Strip,
somewhere near Tower Records
have him in a pose where he peers down,
a grin showing his teeth
over a lectern
swaying back and forth,
like a religious man at prayer
reading poetry.
The billboard would have moving parts,
the mouth moving,
as well as the lectern,
as he sways,
maybe some puffs of smoke,
like the old Camel sign on Broadway,
only this time it would be poetry,
he'd be reading poetry,
like a Chinese dictator
and I'd pull out of a traffic jam,
and head for Fresno
where I'd offer him
the negative.

enough

I wasn't an easy guy
when the kids were young.
We would travel,
I would get uptight,
I would worry about details.
I actually wanted to be alone,
didn't accept that we had a crowd —
you know,
the family,
doing it.
Didn't know how to do stuff like that.
I knew how to work
and I knew how to be with my wife on a vacation,
but, I didn't know how to be with the kids.
It was annoying having to take care of them
and do things for them,
and that annoyed me,
especially during times
when I worked really hard
and wanted to have time for myself.
I didn't create enough of that,
so I'd get annoyed,
and I was annoyed at myself,
and wound up annoyed,
and I was probably not fun during those times.
I'll have to ask the kids.
Was I fun?
And they would probably say,
no, you weren't fun.
And then what do I do?
I can't change it.
All I can do is ride a horse
and try to be funny right now.

Maybe ride the horse backwards,
but I could fall,
and that would be dangerous,
and I don't know how to ride a horse.
The spelling of fun backwards is "nuf,"
and maybe I did enough
and maybe I didn't.

languages

we speak different languages
you and I.
I speak from the fear of a
mountain lion,
and cannot speak
unless I shake
with terror
behind a bush.
It is dark when I speak,
and I cannot come to grips
with the long night
and how difficult it is
to find prey
when I am quiet.

I walked to the computer shop

I walked to the computer shop
last night
don't walk much in LA
usually drive to a place to do an
errand and try to park as close as
possible
when I find an empty meter
I reach into the film
container filled with quarters
and feed the meter
I don't walk far to these stores
the idea is to get as close as
I can
like playing a board game
rolling the dice and moving
one square at a time
racing my opponent to the final
box
last night I parked the car
remembered I
needed to pick up the computer
and turned back to the car
but it was only
two blocks to the store
and decided to walk but the thought
of skipping the car was like
giving my opponent three turns
at the dice
quickly after his move
so I started out walking to the
light waiting for the signal
crossing and turning

at the car wash passing the
liquor store and then to the
computer store
I walked in and gave the clerk
the claim check
when he returned with the computer
I paid
turned to walk home again
and
I thought about my car
and if I had it
I could place the computer
on the front passenger seat
and drive home
couldn't figure out how to carry it
and finally put it under
my arm
as if it were a notebook
and I were walking home from
school
I crossed through the car wash
felt the spray
as a man washed his car
climbed up the incline
to the light at Neilson Way
crossed the street with a biker
heading for the beach
and when I returned home
it felt like the first time I
ventured from home
and returned to
the smell of dinner
my mother touching my
cheek to see if I was really
there

I didn't need the computer
that night and placed it on
the counter as I entered
felt tired after the walk
and sat down to call a friend
to tell him how it was
to be alive again.

Vogel's ears

Vogel attempted to trap his ears. They had been elusive, but he hunted them, and was patient. They alighted from the thick green park above the river. There in the night, he waited. Waited for the sound of the river to halt for just one moment. One moment of silence in that rush. But when the ears came through the night, his eyes began to see. Vogel circled. He knew he had them. He knew if he just waited one more moment, he would be able to capture them, and feel the quiet he yearned for. But a taxi came by just at the moment he was about to close in on his ears. The ears fell back into the woods. Disappeared like a stranger in a crowd. Suddenly gone. Vogel searched and searched. Each tree. Each rock. It would have to be another time. He placed himself above the rocks and waited.

solitude (I)

they come alive
when I'm gone
the low slung chair
sitting at the window
over the ocean
it sits and waits
for me to leave
the smaller chair
next to it
almost touching
waiting patiently
like grandparents
waiting
until I am gone again
then they move
they party
I just know it
their private world
over the ocean
they strut and dance
to the sound of the rocks as they rumble
under the tide
dipping to the light
of the moon
and smiling to the sound of
their song
they jazz to it all
they have this place
to themselves
laughing
singing
dancing
to their song

blue chairs

I drive by my father's retirement home
where he spent the last two years of his life.
I fear passing by
not wanting
to see that place,
not wanting
to remember.
And when I look into the lobby
there are five women on blue chairs
talking to each other.
The next time,
I'll stop,
and ask if they miss him.

the gardener

in a dry wind of tossed feathers and papers curled into brushes
the new gardener arrived and pressed the bell
the light on the phone blinked as I looked out the window
and buzzed him in
I opened the door and he smiled through a round face
deeply tanned with sculpted narrowed eyes
I'm marc the new gardener
we shook hands
his hand was larger than mine rough and hardened
I walked him into the garden
showed him the trees and the plants
and the young tree I was concerned about
he called me sir each time he spoke
and when he did he backed up a step
like a horse before the saddle goes on
he told me he would return in the morning
but later he phoned called me sir
and said he couldn't make it but not to worry
when he does return he'll trim the trees
and the bushes to look natural
full and overflowing
and wild like his hands
I remembered his hands
they were flat and wide like shovels
and his eyes were the deep purple of berries
I remembered what he said about the young tree
how it was in shock put in too young
that it would come back
I'll give it love and shock dirt he said
I didn't know what he meant
but I liked his enthusiasm
and how he smelled of clay in rain
he would plant climbing petunias he said

and variegated ivy
that the sun would not burn the ivy
he reminded me of the wildness of the
gardener in the play I had seen
arcadia
about the gardens of the English countryside
and how the architecture of the garden
reflected the air and the values
how men think and act
and I wondered how the garden
reflected my life
and wondered if I would let it all
grow wild
if this gardener would ever return
and a few days later he called
that he would return in the morning
and again he did not show
I thought he was a fraud or had too much
to do
and wondered if I should forget the whole
thing
but then he returned the next day
unannounced
and trimmed the trees
to let the light in he said
and called me sir again
I'll bring the flowers tomorrow he went on
and I'm sorry for the delay
he asked to be paid and I wrote him a check
but somehow knew he would not return
and wondered if the house would
remember him
if photographs can be taken by walls
and after he left
my mind wandered into a labyrinth

of tall bushes
box-trimmed into a maze
the gardener ran from row to row
and I knew he was lost
but later I found myself at the window again
and decided to wait for
his return
for those deep eyes
and how he called me sir.

brown dog

a brown dog pulled at the tether
snarled
moved forward
then back
paced
under a hut
on the beach
a hut built by surfers

the day was sunny
a mist
over the seam of sand and water
a sailboat quivered
at the dying wind
while a young boy paddled
on a yellow board

suddenly, the dog charged
from under the hut
traveled low on the sand
attacked
my dog
he bit and ran
circled
ready to attack again

a woman ran from under the hut
pulled the snarling dog back
my dog sat and trembled
howled at the bite
I held my dog as I looked at the hut
the tethered dog paced again

I stood and waited for my dog
she rose and walked ahead
I picked up a long stick
held it like a walking stick
but my seething anger
swung at the air
wanting to battle that dog

until my dog
returned
took that stick in her mouth
walked toward home
balancing it, as if on a trapeze
a stick so long
she could not enter the door
and left it on the sand

Vogel and just oatmeal

Vogel sat empty handed. He had delivered the roses. In the gold box. Left it with the maid. The blond. It was raining now. The delivery took no time. He was ahead of schedule. It was a soft rain. The street was glossy. The gray sidewalk, now brown with puddles and dirty sky. The day began early for Vogel. Took the subway to the shop. The first delivery, and now the roses. Her name was Westbrook. I. Westbrook. She wasn't home. The maid reached for the flowers, and gave Vogel a dollar. Vogel had time now. He expected the delivery to take longer. He got on his bicycle. The seat was wet. Vogel slid his raincoat under his butt and pedaled into the street. He rode around the corner to the coffee shop on 97th street. The window of the shop was steamed. He entered and looked around for a seat. He slid onto a stool at the counter, and pulled his arms free from the raincoat. Let it fall back over the stool, the empty sleeves flopped there like a doll. Coffee? Yes, please. Vogel sat behind a display of packaged pound cake. There wasn't much room. He felt crowded, but also warm, as if cared for. The waiter reached over the stack of cakes and placed the coffee in front of Vogel. Hey Irma what'll it be? The woman next to Vogel squeezed her eyes. Make it one egg over easy, and a side of cottage cheese, and whole wheat toast. Irma, Vogel repeated. I haven't heard that name much. Vogel tried to check out her face without trying to be obvious. Irma what? Irma Westbrook. I just delivered flowers to an I. Westbrook. That's me. No kidding. Who from? Me. You? Just kidding. Vogel smiled at her soft white face. He saw scroll work in her features. Like an old brass lock. What's your name? Vogel. Vogel what? Just Vogel. Her thin brown lips parted as she smiled. You're a delivery guy. Yeah. An arm shot out over the top of the cakes, a plate fisted onto the counter in front of the woman. She turned to her breakfast. I wonder who they're from, she repeated quietly. Me, Vogel murmured again. Me. She turned to Vogel. But Vogel stared ahead. What'll it be?, the counterman interrupted. Oatmeal, Vogel answered. Just oatmeal? he repeated. Just oatmeal, Vogel said.

waiting for the plane

confusion
fog
airplanes
people
Oakland
Seattle
bags
heavy
shops
lit up
shoulders tired
baby in red
monitors
lights
delays
departures
arrivals
tickets
ID
large bags
cavernous halls
people everywhere
like in China
in the subway
pushed in
at a slant
like candles
all burning together

the scarf

I'm sick with a tickle in my throat
as if I swallowed sandpaper
as if the sirens became caught in there after a fire
as if the car battery choked on gas
and dried on a river bed
as if mountains came loose overnight
and tucked themselves under the covers of my bed
like a lover arranges her pose
to feel the fluid motion of love
and then the rough harsh sounds of morning
and how its edges trickle with dreams
like the long scarf I found in Dublin
in that small basket in the corner of the store
with long fingers of wool
and how it was difficult to buy
because it was August with warm rained air
and how it touches my throat softly
to warm the harsh sounds of this cough
the sting and the yawn reproach of this sneeze
as it enters and lifts me up like a violent wind
and spits me out like an unchewed bone.

retirement home

I clean out the back of my truck
his TV
the books
and the pictures
from my Father's room
the place he called a dump
the retirement home
the rooms of silence
where they sat
and now can't talk about his death
because it surrounds them
and how they always said hello to me
but not now
not after his death
how they are next
and how the subject is taboo
like the night and a bad dream
an unspeakable act
and how to forget it
means opera and singing
and how the long curls are gone from
the woman with the rose
her face like desert wind
and she does not ask me
about his death
my Father's friend
and I realize that she is in her own dream
about space
and the emptiness of sky
and her own death
how it speaks in that dream
like a mourner who wants to forget
and the night, how it stays away

but speaks again and again
and how black it must be.

solitude (II)

Last night the poet said
the reason a poet writes
is not to be alone.
And I wondered what that meant.
Is it how people populate a room
while he writes.
Or how opened doors close after
they leave.
And the aloneness, how does
that bedevil the poet.
How does he live with his poems
and those people
that have no shape but the
page they are on.
No form other than
the verse, and how it is placed there.
And the books he has written
are usually a few.
A thick one that contains them all.
And a few thin ones
with poems that kept him
company
while he wrote them.

still life

He entered the park in Switzerland
where the chess pieces were as large
as the men who moved them.
They walked among the pieces
on a life sized board,
the squares were the size of windows.
And for a moment, in the rain,
the men remained still.
He could not tell who was alive,
as he watched the slow play,
the waiting between moves,
the rain, as it slanted into the
clock face on the building
over the park,
as if it had been crying.
Later, each man left the park separately.
The chess pieces remained on the board,
in play, in the rain.
And it seemed to him that each game
must be replayed again and again,
and sometimes it would have to be
replayed
even in the rain.

markers

At the cemetery today
the preacher said,
peace
comes with death.
Death was all around me there.
A friend inadvertently
stepped on the
face of a buried man pictured
on a bronze plaque hidden
in the grass.
It was a square in
the ground with a name I do
not remember now.
And I wonder if anyone
returns to visit that marker.
If his family remembers him.
And I wonder why my
friend walked on his plaque
and does it matter
this day,
when the wind blows,
and the tall grass hides so many faces.

birthright

Today I search for my
father's *talis* misplaced
in the chaos of his death
and reminded by my brother
how we chipped in to buy it for him
and now wishes to reclaim it as
the eldest son

And I wonder if my brother
wishes to wrap himself
in his own tears about the loss of
our father or perhaps he wants
to hold onto it as a thread to the past
But today I cannot find it
and wonder if it has flown away
to my father who called
for it from his plot in Israel
because he needs it
on cold mornings in that cemetary

And does not want
to mix my brother's tears with
the tears he shed for my mother
And maybe today his arms reach
for more than the *talis*
as he wanders in that cemetary
and talks to his neighbors
Continues to watch over
my mother's grave
Or maybe he and my mother
are planning to remarry after
sixty years and

use the shawl for their
canopy
Or maybe he wants to place it
in a trust for his grandchildren

And maybe today as I look for this
aged patch of wool
I will not find it because it had
its own wings when he died
and flew with him
as I tried to hold it for a moment
to remember how
it wrapped his shoulders
and how he had to fold it
into epulets as if it were
a military uniform
And today he stands
in that cemetary with tears
because he knows my brother
wants his *talis*
the one he wore
to pray for us

---

talis, is a prayer shawl.

Noah's ark

noah's eyes stare at me in
a painting by Picasso
and from the glass
eyes of a carved
angel at the side of
the tub
and in those eyes
I arrive at his mountain
under columns of smoke
where wild animals are
paired into twos
and noah's eyes are as dark
and hard as the wood of
the ark

how large that
vessel seems
and wish I could have been
witness to this adventure
to see how all the species
fit into one ark
and I watch them enter
and see the ramp disappear
the ark float away
and now wonder if the
animals today
remember that voyage or
did it happen too long ago

and if Darwin would have been there to observe the
boarding, would he remove his
hat to wipe his brow as he helps
a turtle he brought along for the

saving, and a lizard that seems
ashamed of its looks, as well as
tropical birds in so much
confusion

and how difficult it would be for
the animals to leave this man
who turns them over to noah
as if they were children off to camp
and how he waves goodbye
and leaves a coin at the site
to remember where the ark
was built

and would Darwin then return to
his home in the Galapagos
and wait for the news of
the voyage and continue his
studies
always wondering about noah
afloat in the world with animals
they both love
and how noah would leave
his ark only to find food
for the animals
and return
with newspapers filled with war.

invisible

this morning there was no time to write
my mother my father past loves trembled
in the long hallway
I rushed to my appointment knowing
I would have to leave them even though
they are long dead
they still speak about me and talk to me
when they can
arrive at the tip of my pen
mother smiles and cups her mouth
to hide her teeth
perhaps to hide the smear of her
lipstick
and her eyeglasses as large as a mask
and my father's long arms under
weary eyes after dinner
his head nodding in his chair
and my mother reminding him
about the dates he does not take
her on
at that he arises and
walks from the room and waves his
hand as if swatting a fly
and later I find him in bed
in an undershirt and boxers
turned onto his side
one arm under his face
as if he were swimming
and cannot speak to him then
or this morning before I left for work
and tonight before I go to sleep
they wait in the hallway
and chat about their grandchildren

and how much it costs to live in Florida
how New York is so cold
and tonight the visit is unending
as they walk between rooms
my mother collects plastic shopping bags
and when she dies we find drawers
filled with crushed plastic bags
emptied of her past
and now I am left with see-through
stories that she told me when I was
young but would not speak of when she
aged
and still waves me away
each time I ask

look at all this

I see a wooden deck
turned silver gray
as if it were the fine
hair of an old man.
A fence held up by twisted
vines.
And at the far end of the garden
I see
a white greenhouse,
and behind that, I see
tall eucalyptus trees
with peeled bark
like kids with
shoelaces untied.
And the cat, I see it run
to the flowers and disappear.
And the charcoal gray sky,
I see it through
a break in the trees with
stars embedded in velvet.
And he wants me to see
all this.
We are outside his home
and I see his arms stretched
in front of him
tortuous
and angry at his wife.

I saw Moses on the elevator

I saw Moses on the elevator
he was older than I remembered
but no beard
just gray stubble on a square jaw

and since we were not in the Desert
he was not in a long flowing robe over sandals
no black stripes on the cotton
and he was shorter too

he wore a blue denim shirt
and his trousers were like
french work pants
black and white checks

his eyes were the pearl gray of mist
black speckles
like linoleum
he averted my stare
and looked up at the
numbers
as if they were stars
and I was embarrassed to ask him
for his autograph
but started to push myself
and when I finally got the nerve
he had already left

and I was disappointed
after all
how often do you see a guy like that
on the same elevator
next time I'll have to speak up

Vogel's yellow yarn

Vogel pulled all the yarn from the ball. As it unravelled for the first time, he picked at it like spaghetti. It was soft. Tangled, and hopelessly yellow. He loved the color. He wanted a sweater that yellow, and that comfortable. He gathered all the yarn, and walked to the knitter. It was a long walk. He passed a fallen doll needing hair, and a lamppost without paint. And a man holding bread, wanted those thick fibers that seemed like more. People turned and pointed at the man with so much yellow yarn. A cat arrived at Vogel's feet, pawed at all the yellow. But Vogel persevered, found the knitter, and entered. The man was old. He sat with a cigarette between his lips. Small gold wired glasses at the end of his nose. He leaned from the glare of the bulb. Eyed Vogel's yarn, and said "I wondered when you would be arriving."

birth

Bring these waves to me this beach
A dog lies down in the ocean bed
Waves trancelike water beats into foam at the
Edge of all this sea
The sea as calm as I have seen it rough
I have seen it surprised by so much wind
It laps a froth of spray at the end of a monstrous wave
A pregnant woman walks by in a bathing suit
She swims her unborn baby inside the womb
A child as sea born as the wildest mammal
And yet when born to man breathing
His air and seeing his sun
Perhaps a dolphin rises to become
That baby to be the sea
To be the earth and hear me old
Tremors hear me as I raise this
Sword of the sea my life conquers
As this baby swims inside his own
Birth water and when someday
He is in flight or on a boat
He remembers the sea how it gurgled
How it mumbled about his face
His arms and legs
And how the fine sand on this beach
Became the footing he first grasps
And how he must endure so much
In this rhythm
Life left behind in the sand
And yet always surfacing again inside
That womb
Wet and dying to live.

Note: Our father wrote this poem right before he was diagnosed in September 1998.

picture in my mind

(by Donna Marlene Josephs)

My eyes will never forget
I see you in front of me
white puffy bandage
dome-like around your head.
Your fluffy blonde hair
hiding.
It's dark in here
in this womb like place.
Quiet.
The soft tones of your
monitors and IV's
hum rhythms into
the air.
Yellowed skin.
Slight shoulders exposed
under the white sheet.
You are warm.
One transparent tear
in your left eye.
"I'm so grateful," you say,
"so grateful."
"I can move everything –
my fingers, my toes.
I can move everything."
I reach across your chest
to hug you.
The bed's metal bar is
in the way.
I hug you the best
I can.
"Thank God, Dad."
"Thank God."

I sit with you
in the ICU unit
for 6 hours that night —
the night you shared
your vulnerability.
It was a privilege to be there
with you, Dad.
I watch you heal.
I am so grateful
that you are healing.

insect

the desert plants on the high porch
tossed in the wind off the ocean
fine branches seem to be the legs
of an insect
yesterday there was an insect
on the wall near my bed
it was still from the moment
I first noticed it
I decided to let it be
before my illness I probably would have
killed it
now life is so precious
and nature so balanced
it is hard to crush a fine
insect
even though there'd be no sounds
were I to do it

Santa Monica parking lot

yesterday the ophthalmologist said that I should not drive
I felt depressed and
low after that
later I thought about the things that are told
to patients about recovery and how miracles
can occur
I decided to accept her expertise for the
moment but I've been a fighter all my life and plan
to fight to ultimately be able to do some
driving even if it's in an empty
Santa Monica parking lot

when I woke up after
the brain surgery and realized
I could move my limbs
the eye condition did not seem to be
a big deal but it's gotten worse and now
stabilized
I fear any future loss

the photograph

(by Donna Marlene Josephs)

Staring at the photograph
I so carefully chose
of Dad.
Healthy, smiling,
face bright,
blue eyes sparkling.
The contrast of his black
shirt, against the
dark background
makes his face even
more radiant.
I place the photo in
an exquisite frame from India
beaded
deep blues,
purples and yellows.
The frame stands proudly on my
white counter.
Is that it?
A life
an entire life
summed up in one picture
in one frame?
Even if I filled my
apartment
with pictures
and beautiful frames
would that be enough
to give honor to Dad's
life?
His twists, turns,
stops and gos?

His breath,
his thoughts,
the songs in
his heart?
No. It is not
enough.
The finite can
never
pay full homage
to the infinite –
the Divine spark
in each of us.
How awesome
we are.
Do we even see it?
We must.
We must see it and live it
and embrace each other
enraptured by the
glory of Being.

the decision

(by Donna Marlene Josephs)

When I decided to move
from New York to L.A.
to be with Dad in the last
months of his life,
I made a decision to
create sweet moments
for both of us.
Moments I would treasure
in my memory and in my heart.
Yes, I read the newspaper to him in the morning,
I read poetry to him on tapes,
I encouraged his friends to visit,
and I listened with an open heart
when he cried.
But the sweetest moments for me
were at night.
After getting Dad down the stairs,
into his pajamas, teeth brushed,
Eva and I would help Dad into bed
into his thick, puffy, white bed covers.
We'd swing his feet to the bottom of the bed
because he couldn't do it himself.
We'd place his head comfortably on his pillow.
Then I'd open my arms and say,
"Okay, Papa Bear, here's your good-night hug."
And he'd stretch his arms out wide,
and wrap them around me
patting my back with his thick fingers.
"I love you, Papa Bear."
"I love you too, Honey."
"Goodnight. You'll have a good, restful sleep, Dad."

"Ok, Honey."
We'd drape the heavy covers over him,
and I'd tuck him in tight
so he would feel nice and snug.
And as the months went on,
my hugs got stronger,
and his arms got weaker.
He couldn't stretch them wide anymore.
They would stay folded
at the elbow
resting gently on his chest.
But we both knew
he did the best he could.
We loved those hugs —
at night.
And I wonder —
Did he feel safe,
even for a moment,
during those hugs
in his white, puffy bed?
Did he feel relief from the
fear and the dread of
what was happening
inside of him?
I hope so.
I hope so.
"I love you, Papa Bear."
"I love you too, Honey."
"Goodnight. You'll have a good restful sleep, Dad."
"Ok, Honey."

keeping warm

I always call my kids.
I love them.
They are on their own
in New York
where I was born.
Where I was raised.
They were brought up out
here in California.
I left New York to be free.
To find out about myself.
To feel better inside.
To get away from the old
to find out about newness
and sunshine and warmth,
and now they are there
in the cold,
warming themselves
on my memories.

www.ingramcontent.com/pod-product-compliance
Lightning Source LLC
Chambersburg PA
CBHW020911090426
42736CB00008B/585